Daisy and Friends

Waiting for the School Bus

By
Barbara J. Meredith

Illustrations by Kalpart

Library of Congress Control Number: 2025913474

ISBN: 979-8-89228-631-2   (Paperback)
ISBN: 979-8-89228-632-9   (Hardcover)
ISBN: 979-8-89228-633-6   (eBook)

Printed in the United States of America

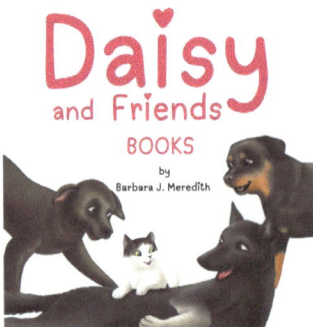

Portions of the proceeds will be donated to: Bandit's Place, Inc. of Connecticut Kitty Angels of Coventry, Connecticut Protectors of Animals, East Hartford, Connecticut

This book is dedicated to my family:
CJ, Mike, Holly and Carson

Hi! My name is Daisy. Meet my three dog friends Smokie, Rocky, and H–Dee. We are waiting for the school bus to bring our friends home from school. Would you like to wait for the school bus with us?

Is this the school bus?
No, this is a dump truck.

A dump truck is for moving heavy loads,
with a back part that can be raised at one
end so that its contents fall out.

Is this the school bus?
No, this is a fire truck.

A fire truck is a vehicle that carries firefighters and equipment for putting out large fires. When it's on its way to a fire, it blares a loud noise which tells all the other vehicles to move out of the way so it can get to the fire faster. Can you make the sound a fire truck does?

Is this the school bus?
No, this is a low bed truck carrying a bulldozer.

A low bed truck has a trailer designed to carry heavy equipment and machinery. A bulldozer is a powerful tractor with a broad upright blade at the front for clearing the ground.

Is this the school bus?
No, this is a city transit bus.

A transit bus is a vehicle made to carry many passengers throughout the city to get them from place to place.

Is this the school bus?
No, this is an oil delivery truck.

An oil delivery truck carries heating fuel to a person's home or business so their house stays warm when it's cold outside.

Is this the school bus?
No, this is a bucket truck.

A bucket truck lifts a worker in a bucket high in the air to repair telephone wires, to cut down tall trees, and to work on the roofs of buildings and homes.

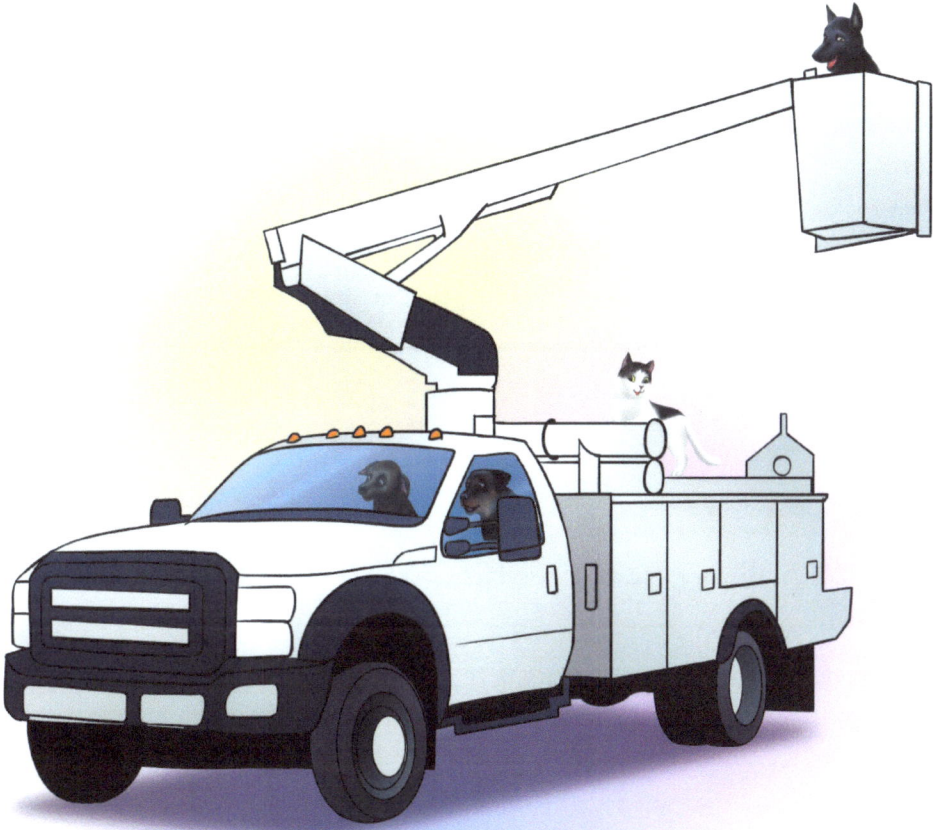

Is this the school bus?
No, this is a police car.

A police car is a vehicle that police officers use to patrol cities and towns and keep people safe.

Is this the school bus?
No, this is a motorcycle.

A motorcycle is a two-wheeled vehicle that is
powered by a motor and can carry
only one or two passengers.

Is this the school bus?
No, that is a garbage truck.

A garbage truck is used to take people's garbage
away to a dump or recycling center.

Is this the school bus?
No, that is a mail delivery truck.

A mail truck is used to carry letters and packages
to a person's home or business.

Is this the school bus?
No, this is a tow truck.

A tow truck is used to pull broken or damaged vehicles.

Is this the school bus?
Yes, this is the school bus!

A school bus transports children to and from school. We can't wait to hear about our friend's day at school.

www.ingramcontent.com/pod-product-compliance
Ingram Content Group UK Ltd.
Pitfield, Milton Keynes, MK11 3LW, UK
UKHW050916090925

7773UKWH00047B/53